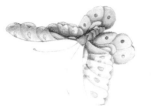

# Grandmother
# Remembers

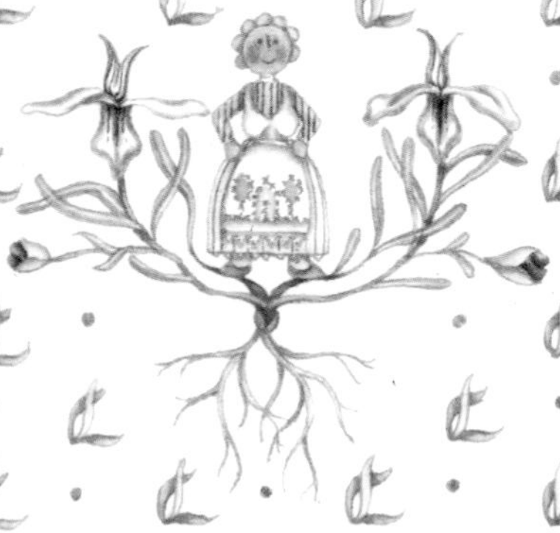

# Grandmother Remembers

## A Written Heirloom for My Grandchild

*Conceived and written by Judith Levy*
*Designed and illustrated by Judy Pelikan*

A Welcome Book

Stewart, Tabori & Chang, Publishers, New York

Edited by Marya Dalrymple

43rd Printing

Published in 1983 and distributed in the United States by
Stewart, Tabori & Chang, a division of U.S. Media Holdings, Inc.
575 Broadway, New York, NY 10012. Distributed in Canada by General Publishing
Company Limited, 30 Lesmill Road, Don Mills, Ontario, M3B 2T6, Canada.
Distributed in the U.K. by Hi Marketing, 38 Carver Road, London SE24 9LT, England.
Distributed in Europe by Onslow Books Limited, Tyler's Court, 111A Wardour Street,
London W1V 3TD, England. Distributed in Australia and New Zealand by
Peribo Pty Limited, 58 Beaumont Road, Mount Kuring-gai NSW 2080.

Printed and bound in Japan

*I offer you my memories*
*So that you will know*
*Your Grandmother was a little girl*
*Not so long ago.*

With love for _____

From _____

Date _____

# Table of Contents

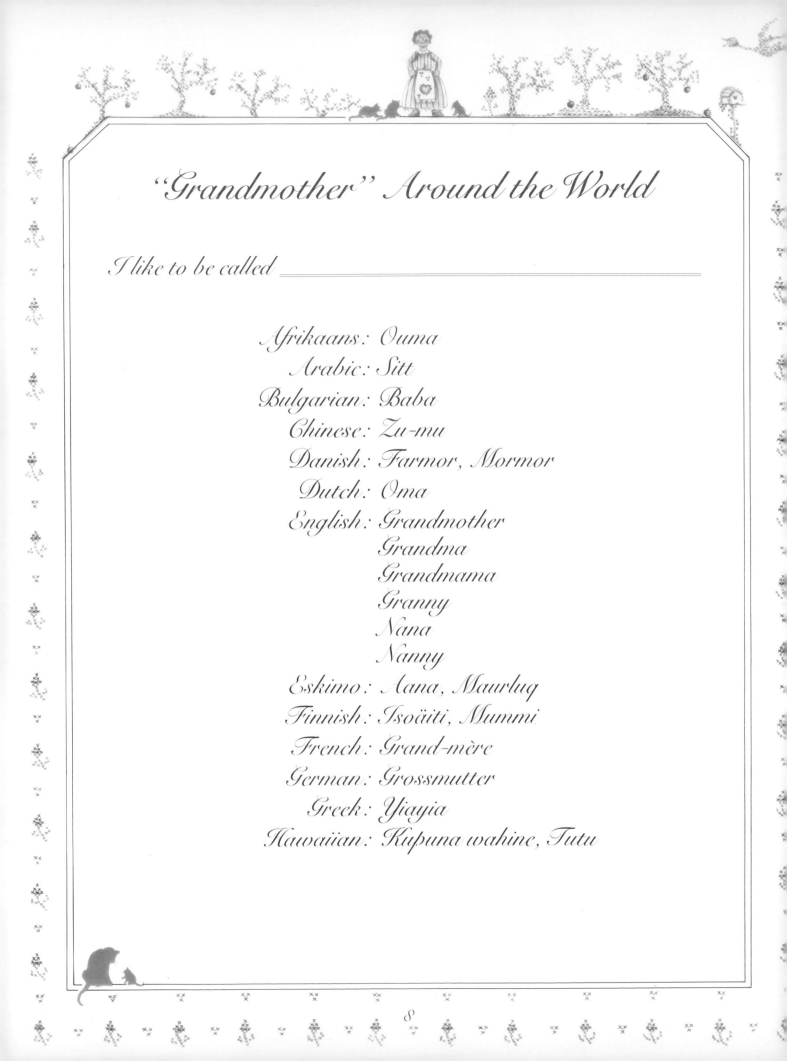

# "Grandmother" Around the World

I like to be called _____

Afrikaans: Ouma
Arabic: Sitt
Bulgarian: Baba
Chinese: Zu-mu
Danish: Farmor, Mormor
Dutch: Oma
English: Grandmother
Grandma
Grandmama
Granny
Nana
Nanny
Eskimo: Aana, Maurluq
Finnish: Isoäiti, Mummi
French: Grand-mère
German: Grossmutter
Greek: Yiayia
Hawaiian: Kupuna wahine, Tutu

Hebrew: Savta
Hungarian: Nagyanana
Irish: Mama, Seanmháthair
Italian: Nonna
Japanese: Oba-San
Korean: Hal Mo-ni
Norwegian: Farmor, Mormor
Polish: Babcia
Portuguese: Avó
Romanian: Bunica
Russian: Babushka
Spanish: Abuela, Abuelita
Swahili: Nyanya
Swedish: Farmor, Mormor
Turkish: Büyük anne
Vietnamese: Bà
Welsh: Mam-gu, Nain
Yiddish: Bobe
Zulu: Ukhulu, Isalukazi

# Our Family Tree

You, my little apple,
Sprang from a sturdy tree.
Branches of generations
Embrace you tenderly.

Great Grandmother

Great Grandmother

Great Grandmother

Great Grandfather

Great Grandfather

Great Grandfather

Great Grandmother

Great Grandfather

Grandfather

Grandmother

Grandfather

Grandmother

Mother

Father

Name

# My Grandparents

## My Mother's Family

My Grandfather's name _____

My Grandmother's name _____

My Grandparents came from _____

They settled in _____

My Grandfather earned his living _____

_____

My Mother was born on _____

## My Father's Family

My Grandfather's name _____

My Grandmother's name _____

My Grandparents came from _____

They settled in _____

My Grandfather earned his living _____

_____

My Father was born on _____

*Photograph of
Grandmother's Parents*

# My Parents

*The dearest friends in life*
*A little girl ever had*
*Were the two special people*
*I called "Mom" and "Dad."*

My Father's name _____

My Mother's name _____

My parents met

How _____

_____

_____

When _____

_____

Where _____

_____

They were married

Date _____

Place _____

My Father earned his living _____

_____

*Photograph of
Grandmother as a Baby*

# I Was Born

*About the day that I was born*
*There's much that I don't know.*
*But here are just a few facts*
*My Mother said were so.*

I was born

    When _____

    Where _____

I was named _____

That name was chosen because _____

_____

_____

I weighed _____

I was told I resembled _____

_____

My brothers' and sisters' names _____

_____

*Photograph of
Grandmother
as a Young Girl*

# As a Young Girl

*Life is like a rosebud*
*Waiting to unfold.*
*Each petal is a story*
*Waiting to be told.*

My family lived _____

_____

I went to school _____

_____

As a student I _____

_____

My ambition was _____

_____

_____

At home I was expected to _____

_____

My parents were very strict about _____

_____

_____

My Father taught me to value _____

_____

My Mother taught me to value _____

_____

What I loved most about my Father was _____

_____

What I loved most about my Mother was _____

_____

My teenage years were _____

_____

_____

# As a Girl "My Favorite…"

Song _____

Movie _____

Actor _____

Actress _____

Book _____

Radio program _____

Season _____

Vacation spot _____

Holiday _____

Flower _____

Color _____

Sport _____

Food _____

Subject in school _____

Friend _____

# As a Young Woman

I was graduated from _____
   Date _____
After I finished school I _____
_____

I worked as _____
_____

On weekends I _____
_____

The fashion rage at the time was _____
_____

_____

I started to date at the age of _____
I met your Grandfather at _____
_____

His full name _____
His birthday _____
His heritage _____

Our first date was _____

_____

_____

His age when we met was _____

He lived _____

I lived _____

He earned his living _____

_____

I liked him because _____

_____

_____

Grandfather said he liked me because _____

_____

_____

When we dated we liked to go _____

_____

_____

# My Engagement

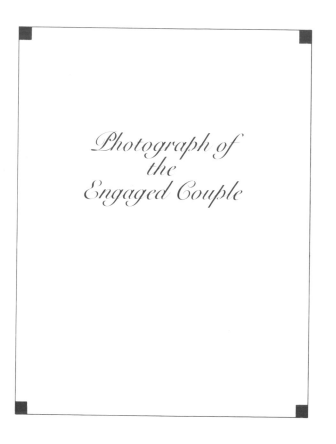

*Photograph of
the
Engaged Couple*

Of all the men in the world
I knew he was the best,
So when Grandfather asked to marry me,
I happily said, "Yes!"

Our courtship lasted _____

When I told my parents they _____

_____

We became engaged on _____

When Grandfather proposed he said _____

_____

_____

*Photograph of
Grandmother as a Bride*

# My Wedding Day

*I put my hand in his hand,*
*As we stood side by side,*
*On that very special day*
*When I became a bride.*

Grandfather and I were married

Date _____

Time _____

Place _____

I wore _____

We celebrated our wedding by _____

_____

_____

Our most memorable wedding gift was _____

_____

My most vivid memory of my wedding day is _____

_____

_____

After we married we traveled to _____

_____

*Photograph of*
*Grandmother*
*and Grandfather*
*as a*
*Young Couple*

# My First Year of Marriage

When Grandfather and I were first married we lived in _____
_____
_____

We lived there for _____
My fondest memory of our first home is _____
_____
_____
_____

Grandfather's job was _____
_____

After we married I _____
_____
_____

When we took trips, we liked to go _____
_____
_____

As a wife I tried to be _____
_____
_____

*Photograph of
Grandmother and Baby*

# Your Parent Was Born

*The day I had a baby*
*Surely changed my life.*
*We were now a family;*
*I was a Mother and a Wife.*

Your parent was born

When _____

Where _____

We lived at _____

Full name _____

We chose that name because _____

_____

Color of eyes at birth _____

Color of hair at birth _____

Weight at birth _____

I thought my baby resembled _____

Brothers' and sisters' names _____

_____

Favorite toy was _____

First word was _____

Sometimes we used the nickname _____

I still smile when I think about the time _____

_____

_____

*Photograph of
Grandmother and
Young Child*

# My Child Growing Up

*The growing years were busy,*
*Speeding swiftly by.*
*A decade went past*
*In the blinking of an eye.*

Schools attended were _____

_____

_____

Best subject in school was _____

_____

Showed talent in _____

_____

Ambition was _____

_____

Hobbies were _____

_____

# My Child's Teenage Years

Favorite type of music was _____

_____

Favorite sport was _____

Major interests were _____

_____

Household duties were _____

Spare time was spent _____

_____

Dating began at the age of _____

I set a curfew of _____

I was strict about _____

_____

I was very proud that _____

_____

What I remember most about those teenage years is _____

_____

_____

_____

*Photograph of Teenager*

*Photograph of
the Young Couple*

# Your Parents

## They Met

How _____

_____

_____

_____

When _____

Where _____

_____

_____

## They Were Married

Date _____

Place _____

_____

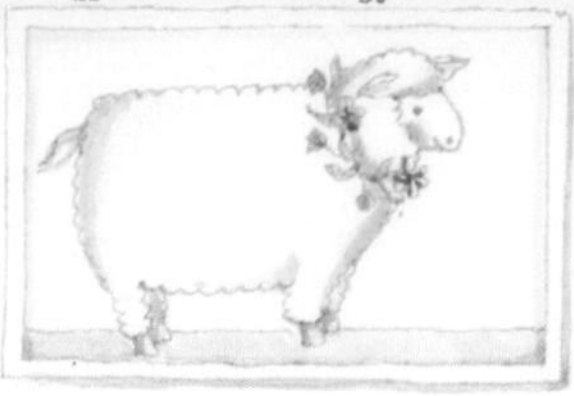

*Photograph of*
*Grandchild as a Baby*

# Your Birth

*The day you were born*
*All my dreams came true.*
*I'm the proudest Grandmother*
*To have a Grandchild like you.*

You were born

When _____

Where _____

When I first heard the news I _____

_____

I thought you resembled _____

_____

When I brag about you I always say _____

_____

# When Our Family Gets Together

*Heritage is more precious
With every passing day.
Traditions keep us close,
In a very special way.*

We always recall the time _____

_____

_____

We fondly laugh about _____

_____

We still remember when you _____

_____

_____

I am happy that we all _____

_____

_____

_____

_____

*I think our family is special because* _____

_____

_____

*The first holiday you shared with us was* _____

_____

Photograph of Our Family

# Holiday Traditions

Holiday _____

Date or season _____

We celebrate this holiday by _____

_____

_____

The special foods served are _____

_____

Holiday _____

Date or season _____

We celebrate this holiday by _____

_____

_____

The special foods served are _____

_____

Holiday _____

Date or season _____

We celebrate this holiday by _____

_____

The special foods served are _____

_____

Holiday _____

Date or season _____

We celebrate this holiday by _____

_____

The special foods served are _____

_____

# Family Recipes

*Grandmother taught my mother*
*And my mother taught me*
*These delicious family recipes*
*I offer lovingly.*

*A Family Favorite* _____

*Ingredients and Directions* _____

_____

_____

_____

_____

_____

_____

_____

_____

_____

_____

_____

_____

*A Family Favorite* _____
*Ingredients and Directions* _____

_____

_____

_____

_____

_____

_____

_____

_____

*A Family Favorite* _____
*Ingredients and Directions* _____

_____

_____

_____

_____

_____

_____

_____

_____

# Dear Relatives

I'd like to help identify
So it's really clear,
Some members of our family
Who are so very dear.

Name

Relationship

Photograph

Name

Relationship

Photograph

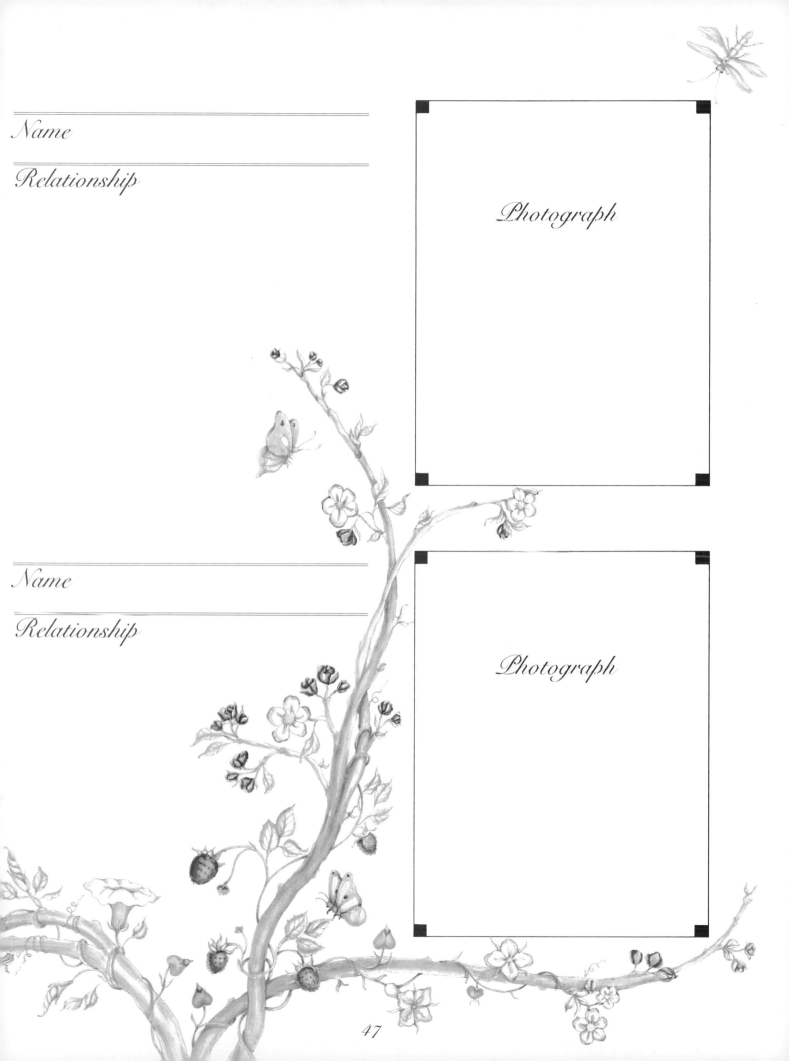

Name

Relationship

Photograph

Name

Relationship

Photograph

*Photograph of
Grandmother Today*

I was naughty when I was little,
I got into mischief too,
But my Grandmother always loved me,
And I'll always love you.

# Thoughts I'd Like to Share with You

*Because you are so dear to me,*
*To you I will reveal*
*Special thoughts, from my heart,*
*Of how I truly feel.*

My deepest values are _____

_____

_____

I was proud of _____

_____

_____

Everyone thought I shouldn't, but I was glad I _____

_____

_____

I was in for a complete surprise when _____

_____

_____

A matter of concern was _____

_____

_____

_____

I was always sorry I didn't _____

_____

_____

_____

I felt very strongly about _____

_____

_____

_____

_____

I've changed my mind, and now I think _____

_____

_____

_____

# How the World Has Changed Since I Was a Little Girl

They invented _____

_____

They discovered _____

_____

They succeeded in preventing _____

When man landed on the moon I _____

A time saver my mother never had is _____

_____

*Women today* _____

_____

*Movies today* _____

_____

*Dating today is different because* _____

_____

_____

*I still like the old-fashioned ways of* _____

_____

_____

*I think the younger generation is wiser about* _____

_____

*I think a woman president would be* _____

_____

# Today "My Favorite..."

Song _____

Movie _____

Actor _____

Actress _____

Book _____

Television program _____

Newscaster _____

Season _____

Vacation spot _____

Holiday _____

Flower _____

Color _____

Dessert _____

Saying _____

_____

# The Future

*Someday you'll have a Grandchild*
*And you will surely see*
*Why being your Grandmother*
*Means the world to me.*

*My wish for the future is* _____

_____

_____

_____

_____

_____

_____

_____

_____

_____

_____

_____

*Photograph of Grandfather*

# Grandfather Would Want You to Know

# I Forgot to Mention

# Treasures I Have Saved for You

My story would be incomplete
Without these souvenirs.
Precious little keepsakes
I've treasured all these years.